THE

HIGHLAND

GAMES

A Beginner's Guide to History, Kilts & Throwing

GARETH AINSWORTH

The Highland Games
Copyright 2020 **Gareth Ainsworth**

Edited by Jessica Ainsworth
Cover Design by 100 Covers
Cover Photo by Kristin Bishop
Author Photograph by
        Todd I. Mason Jr., Capture Essence Photography
Map by BMR Williams
Formatting & Typesetting by Black Bee Media

ISBN: 978-1-7356885-6-5 (Paperback)
         978-1-7356885-5-8 (Ebook)

BEFORE STARTING ANY EXERCISE OR NUTRITION PROGRAM, PLEASE CONSULT YOUR DOCTOR. BY TRAINING WITHIN THIS PROGRAM, OR FOLLOWING ANY OF THE TECHNIQUES, YOU REALIZE AND TAKE FULL RESPONSIBILITY FOR THE RISKS INVOLVED WITH PERFORMING THE FOLLOWING SPORT AND SPECIFIC RECOMMENDED TECHNIQUES.

While the author has made every effort to ensure that the ideas, statistics, and information presented in this book are accurate to the best of his/her abilities, any implications direct, derived, or perceived, should only be used at the reader's discretion. The author cannot be held responsible for any personal or commercial damage arising from communication, application, or misinterpretation of the information presented herein.

Internet addresses given in this book were accurate at the

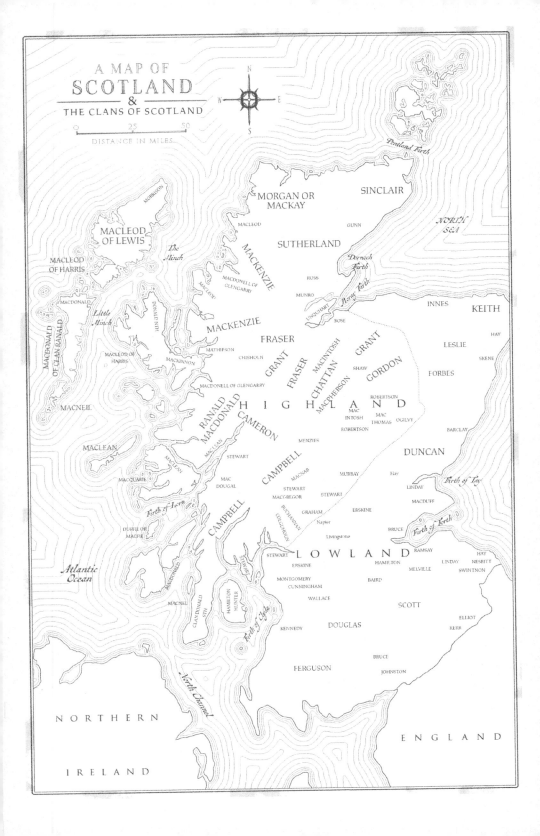

Acknowledgements

Life is about choices and building your circle of influence. Whether it be positive or negative, that is the choice we make.

In the past few years of my life I have grown in many ways and have chosen to pursue a much more positive life in both growth, strength and reflection.

For this I must thank my circle. My wife most of all for being my partner and pushing me to grow and try something different. Because of her, you are reading this book!

To Bill Fredericks and the Penn's Wall Games, my first Highland Games experience and the beginning of an ever growing passion for community, history and strength

My friends in The Old Bay Highlanders. Thank you for the guidance, the training, the feedback and of course the whisky!

Thank you to Kristin Bishop and Jesse Morgan, your photography provided the cover art and the artwork for this book.

And to all those I have enjoyed time with along the way, Cheers!

Contents

Introduction

Welcome to *The Highland Games: A Beginner's Guide to History, Kilts and Throwing.*

Whether you're thinking of getting started in the Games, have a general interest in it, or perhaps, you've been watching the 4th season of The Crown, we're glad you're here. This book is meant to introduce you and hopefully set you on your journey to loving the Games as much as I do. Well, maybe not as much as I do, but you get the point.

The Highland Games has been a journey for me, as it has for many. It's given me so much in my short time throwing. I have discovered a passion, an outlet and a community that embodies the spirit of the highlands and the betterment of their fellow human beings. It's a really uplifting and empowering sport for both spectators and athletes alike.

For over a thousand years, this incredible sport has survived so much and continues to thrive throughout the world today.

This book will take you through the history of the Highland Games, fill you in on all of the events (what they are, who governs them, the different roles, etc.) and how to get started in them. You'll also learn about another important part of the Games and of history... the Kilt. I'll walk you through how to find your family's tartan, where to buy a kilt, how to wear it and I'll cover some of the accessories such as the sgian dubh and the sporran.

I've also started a podcast to help you continue learning and growing past this book, where we also talk to many Heavy Athletes and others within the community about their own stories and experiences in this great tradition. The Kilted Patriot podcast is available on Apple Podcasts, Google Podcasts, Spotify, and more! Check it out here:

https://anchor.fm/kiltedpatriot

The History of the Highland Games

For Centuries, the Scottish Highland Games have been considered to be one of Scotland's greatest cultural exports. Through a display of culture, heritage, strength and freedom, the Games offer activities that every family member can enjoy. Over a thousand years ago warriors would gather and test themselves in feats of strength. Through sheer defiance and determination through oppression, this time-honored traditions and the ancient values would be upheld. The Highland Games continue throughout the world to this day. The events include activities from heavy athletics, dancing, drumming, and piping that pay homage to Celtic and Scottish culture and as always, delicious food and whiskey.

However, where the Games began is often a point of contention. The Tailteann Games ran from 1820 BC to 1180 AD in Ireland. However, Scotland gives credit to King Malcolm III. In 1040 AD Malcolm, in need of a courier, summoned men from different backgrounds to a hill race. The goal of this activity was simple: the fastest man would be his messenger. As well as the honor of the newly bestowed position, the prize also included a purse of gold and a sword. Legend has it that three brothers joined the race and were favored to win. At the start of the race, the two elder brothers took the lead with the youngest lagging behind, begging the king to allow him to race. The king told him that he may but was too far behind to have a chance at winning. However, the youngest brother was quick to catch up and most impressive at running the hill. As he closed the gap between himself and his brothers, it is said he called out, "halves brothers, and I will yield." The brothers responded with a hard no. So, as they became exhausted at the crest of the hill the younger brother darted past. At the same time one of the older brothers fell and grabbed his brother's kilt as he passed, not knowing whether this was to stall his adversary or to save himself from the fall. The youngest brother ripped off his kilt and continued taking the win au naturel. Since then, hill racing continues to play a major role in many Highland Games events. However, people tend to keep their kilts on these days.

According to several experts, the Ceres Games are one of the oldest testaments of Highland Games. The relentless drive of the Scottish people to keep their ceremonious tradition has stood against the test of times, which saw the Games get increasingly popular. The Ceres Games are said to have begun in 1314 – the reason? A Scottish tribute to the people of Fife who had the heart to fight at Bannockburn.

The Battle of Bannockburn took place on the 24th of June in the year 1314. The Scottish pulled off a major victory against the English. Outnumbered by almost 10,000 Englishmen, King Robert the Bruce had dug trenches and laid iron spikes throughout the battleground to hinder Edward II's advancing army. Once the English entered the trap, the Scot's descended upon them fighting into the night. The next day the Scot's were already prepared to attack the tired English encampment, a brave cavalry charge by the Earl of Gloucester was devastated upon the unbroken spears of the Scots.

Bruce's 8,000 men were experienced warfighters. However, with such overwhelming odds, the people of Fife, mainly farmers, had proudly offered their services to the cause. Armed with only rudimentary weapons and King Robert's unwillingness to put them in unnecessary danger, Robert kept the 600 Fifers in reserve and out of sight of the English. However, upon the cavalry charge

King Robert shouted "On them! On Them". The Fifers hearing this cry, immediately descended the hill into the Fray. The English seeing what looked like fresh troops retreated in haste.

Victorious, the Fifer's returned home and were given the freedom of Ceres where a Games was held in their honor. The Scottish National Anthem, The Flower of Scotland, also pays tribute to this incredible victory; "The Flower of Scotland had stood against them, Proud Edward's army, and sent him homeward to think again" This war is considered to be the first war for Scottish Independence.

However, the Highland Games in Cowal are still considered to be the largest gathering in. These Games take place in Dunoon, Scotland every year in August. These Games see the largest crowd gathering and have also been widely publicized for staying true to Scottish culture. In *America* some of the largest gatherings and Games are held in Northern Carolina, and in San Francisco by the Caledonian Club are a pleasant family-outing day, too.

Through the passage of time, Scotland and, incidentally the Games, have faced several hurdles. The Battle of Culloden is one of those instances. The Stuart standard was raised at the Braemar gathering on the 6th of September 1715, beginning the Jacobite Rebellion. Parliament responded with the Disarming Act of 1716, the success of which was shown by the number of antiquated weapons at the beginning of the 1745 rebellion with Charles Edward Stuart. The final battle ever to be held on British soil was at Culloden. On the 16th of April 1746, approximately 7,000 Jacobites faced 8,000 men serving in the British Army, led by The Duke of Cumberland, William Augustus. In just a few short hours, the Jacobites were defeated, with over 1,500 dead or wounded and only 300 casualties to the British.

This a crushing defeat that sent Bonnie Prince Charlie

back into exile. The aftermath resulted in the almost complete destruction of Highland Culture. The British victors gave no quarter and for two days searched the moor, executing anyone found still alive. Later over 1,000 more Jacobites were either executed, banished or transported to the Colonies. The Proscription Act of 1746 furthered the Disarmament, making weapons of any kind a punishable offence, effectively ending hunting. The wearing of kilts, tartan and plaid, speaking Gaelic, bagpipes and any gatherings or Games were all banned as well. The British furthered the humiliation by forcing Clansmen to take the following oath;

> *"I . .... do swear I have not, nor shall have in my possession, any gun, sword, pistol or arm whatsoever, and never use tartan, plaid, or any part of the Highland garb: and if I do, may I be cursed in my undertakings, may I never see my wife or children or relatives: may I be killed in battle as a coward, and lie without Christian burial in a strange land far from the graves of my kindred."*

It was not until 1782 that this Act was repealed. However, parliament and authorities remained suspicious, for many years after, of Scotsmen gathering in any capacity as they were fully aware that the Rebellion which began at Braemar had been under the guise of a gathering for sport.

The version of the Games that people have grown to celebrate currently only started to take form later in the 18th and 19th centuries. During the 18th century, several of the celebratory cultures were abolished. Some were intentionally put to an end, in which others faced societal disruptions and changing generally accepted norms. This phase also showed how the Games used to be a way of life for some people. As the Games saw resistance, seasoned veterans sought other ways of living, because their social status was also taking a hit. For these people, hiring clansmen of the past for Highland Regiments seemed rewarding.

As the Scottish people moved around the world, their cultural influence grew and spread over time. Caledonian societies were formed in the United States, New Zealand, and Canada, and wherever the Scots met in the world, they stuck together and formed a society. After the first Highland Games in New York in 1836, the event was closely followed by a Caledonian Club in San Francisco, which held their first Games in 1866. This tradition continued and now Caledonian clubs can be found in multiple countries around the world.

Nowadays, just like in ancient times, the Highland Games are a mixture of events. Whether it's track, dance, or displays of strength like the tug-o-war or the caber-toss, the organizer's try their best to keep the Games genuine to this day. Such was the popularity that in 1838, Queen Victoria graced the Highland Games with her presence. Her approval and fondness for the Games resulted in a massive surge in popularity for the Highland Games.

Her fondness and appearance at the Games brought about a new tradition for the royal family, that still continues on. Members of the royal family such as Queen Elizabeth II have attended the Games regularly. In 1889, due to a gradual increase in viewership, the International Olympic Committee started to take notice.

Games such as the Shot Put, Hammer Throw, and Tug-O-War were added to the Olympics, *because of the Highland Games.*

The management committee has always focused on making the Games a family event. This social gathering is often an unofficial family reunion for many, where they can enjoy the great food and heavy athletics together. To keep the Scottish tradition alive amidst global attention, the Scottish Highland Games Association made it compulsory for all athletes to wear kilts.

However, even though the Scottish tradition has been kept alive, human physicality tests have greatly evolved. And since the sole purpose of the Games was originally to recognize amazing humans, the Games now have a modern twist.

Some of the more modern additions to the Games include:

- Cycling
- Marathon Races
- Sheep-Dog Trials
- Wellie-Throwing Contests

The traditional Games that were loved by the masses have stuck around, and they are still the Games that viewers are most interested in.

Registrations for the Games are simple; participants can register in three different categories:

- Youth
- Adult
- Senior

To enter the Heavy Athletic Competitions, athletes are broken down into four different categories (we'll get into this a bit more in the coming chapters):

- Amateurs
- Professionals
- Masters
- 190 pounds and below

These categories also include women's classes.

The Tradition of Folk Dance: Not Just for the Ladies

Another popular event at the Games is the folk dance and square dancing have their roots in Highland culture. Back in the 11th and 12th century, the dance was a form

of celebration by the soldiers. (The New Zealand Haka comes to mind as well - if you're not sure what that is, do yourself a favor and head over to YouTube.)

Celebratory dances by the males featured dances performed with swords and shields. Rather than just being a celebration, the dance by the Scottish men was also their way of developing their stamina and priming themselves for war. According to them, these movements made them agile and this culture has continued to this day. It wasn't until Victorian Britain decided to revive this vibrant culture and made it a competition just for men. By the end of the century, women became an essential part of this competition, too. With time this style of dancing was refined greatly, and it transformed into classical ballet.

However, dancing wasn't *only* used for celebrations. Various accounts in history also show that mercenaries of that time used dancing as a plot to assassinate Swedish King John III. They performed this dance at the Stockholm Castle in the year 1753, and the weapons that were used in their dances *just* happened to be a part of the dancing customs. But unfortunately for the Scottish, the plan did not work. These sword dances continued as they were yet again presented in front of Anne of Denmark in 1589 and James VI in 1617. In 1617. The dance was also performed for Charles I while the dancers floated on a raft in the River Tay.

The "Highland Fling" was famously performed at the end of a battle. Male warriors used their Targes (small shield carried to battle) and danced on the battlefield to celebrate their triumph. This dance is based on a stag because the men dancing raised their fingers in the air depicting the antlers of the animal. The Sword Dance according to several historians is also one form of a celebratory dance.

The dance called Sean Triubhas dates back to 1745. Bonnie Prince Charlie challenged England at Culloden and faced heavy defeat. As a form of punishment, the people of the Highlands were barred from wearing kilts ever again. This dance was developed when Scottish people got their right to wear their kilts again due to the Proscription Appeal. They also won their right to play their bagpipes. In this dance, the movements can clearly be seen as the Scottish people shed off their despised trousers and embrace their beloved kilts again. Some of the steps in the dance come from hard shoe dancing which is not a surprise since those are the shoes people would've worn if they wanted to wear shoes at all while dancing.

The Scottish Lilt is a dance form that is performed by the women. This is a courting dance performed by women to show how they can be elegant and graceful just like the Earl of Errol. This dance initially was a hard shoe dance that came into existence because of Aberdeenshire.

Highland Games in America

The Highland Games are held all across North America. The Games today remember the culture and heritage for Scotland in the American people, past and future together. They transport the people watching to Scotland where they can rejoice with the Scottish people to celebrate Celtic and Scottish heritage. Just like Scotland, the Games in America focus on all of the events that are a part of the original Highland Games.

In the Games across America, you're easily going to find an extensive collection of Celtic and Scottish merchandise. People often collect these items as souvenirs to show to their loved ones that they attended the festival. Food and gifts can also be bought from the tents that are present to depict Scottish culture. (Have you ever tried Haggis or Scotch Eggs?!) For the Scottish and Celtic people in America, these Games are an excellent way to rejoice in their memories of Scotland and embrace the culture, the heritage and the community.

Since the first Highland Games event in 1836, they've continued to happen regularly. Over 200 gatherings of the Highland Games annually take place across the U.S., the U.K., and Canada. As a family centric event, families in the U.S. often use the Games to introduce their younger generations to raw Scottish culture.

Keeping the Highland Games Alive

Widespread love and appreciation for the Highland Games have kept them alive throughout the ages. The love of the Highland Games is celebrated all around the world - not just in Scotland. They are a beautiful display of culture, talent and athleticism.

From practices with like-minded individuals to backyard Games and traditional competitions, there is no doubt that the community is strong within the Highland Games.

Highland Games: Events

What exactly is the Highland Games? Back in the day the Games were used as a series of events during Clan gatherings as a chieftains way of selecting the best his Clan had to offer. As we just covered the history of the Highland Games, let's focus on what the Games are today.

Today, this amazing tradition continues all around the world and just as each clan has its own tartan, many of these games also carry their own uniqueness also. While generally all Caledonian Societies and or Heavy Athletic Associations follow Scotland's lead when it comes to the rules, the following are the traditional events you will see.

In each of the following events, every competitor is given three throws, and for the weight over bar and sheaf, athletes may choose their starting height and will be given three attempts at every height they miss. The best of the three throws, or the best height is what is counted and scored for the comp etition.

Toss the Caber

One of the most renowned event's is the Caber Toss. The athletes display their expertise in control, balance, technique, and strength. Although this event is a definite fan and crowd favorite, its roots are generally unknown. The word Caber is derived from the Gaelic CABAR, meaning wooden beam.

According to some, the Scotts used the technique of tossing the caber to bridge the gap between fast-flowing rivers or streams. At the same time, some say that men of the past used this technique to throw big logs on a castle's wall to damage the defense system of the castle.

There may also be other renditions of explanations that we might never know – so we've taught ourselves to love the game as it is. The caber itself is a full-length log. Its length is usually between 15 to 20 feet, and it can weigh from about 100 to 180 pounds. The variation in weight exists because the caber is a tree trunk. Since a tree trunk cannot be a standard size, the dimensions can differ. However, that makes it easy for the different classes of athlete to have a proportionate caber.

As part of Scottish tradition, local trees are utilized to make cabers for the prestigious event. The trees themselves can be of different types such as the Larch or the Scottish Pine.

The How

To take part, according to the game's rules, the participants must cup the log in their hands and then balance it using their body. To make sure the log is holdable in both palms, one end of the log is tapered so that it can easily fit in the hands. Once the athlete has balanced the log using their hands and their body, they then move forward some distance and use the building momentum and their strength to throw the log in the air. The aim of throwing the log into the air is to throw the other end in line with the participant's run. The top end of the log *must* hit the ground first. The lower end then follows, end over end which brings the log to the ground.

To a spectator, the distance and height the log is thrown can be amazing since these logs are massive and heavy. But the judges are not impressed by either of these factors. Judging is based on the position the log comes to rest in after the athlete's throw. For an ideal throw, every athlete aims to throw the caber end over end, directly in front of their run. Scoring is based on the face of a clock. If you're standing at 6 o'clock, for a perfect throw, you have to make the log rest at 12 o'clock after you've thrown it. For the times the caber does not completely flip, judging is based on the angle of up to 90 degrees.

Hammer Throw: Light and Heavy

From the militaristic and warlike roots of Scottish culture, the Hammer Throw is an essential event to the Highland Games. Its roots go way back to the thirteenth century. According to some, the hammer throw was created in response to the English King, Edward I's decision to ban Scots from owning weapons. Since Longshanks didn't classify the hammer as a weapon, clansmen quickly started using the useful tool as such.

But do not confuse "hammer," with what we commonly call the modern-day tool – the event doesn't exactly use what *we* call a hammer. The tool being used in the game is a four-foot-two-inch rod that has a metal ball attached to the end of it, imagine a cannonball on a stick! But like every other tool being used in the games, the Scottish Highland Games Association has guidelines on the hammers that may be used in the event.

The hammer handle is made from wood or cane. In the US a PVC handle is acceptable.

The How

The Hammer Throw consists of both a light *and* heavy hammer, weighing at 16 and 22lbs. Participant's hold the pole, and perform rotational swings around their body, the hammer is released over the shoulder and judges measure the distance. Often, competitors opt for wearing gloves or using a sticky substance known as "tacky" for better grip during the throw, or the use of bladed boots to keep their feet planted, allowing them to lean back much further.

One of the most prominent differences between a Scottish Hammer Throw and an Olympic Hammer Throw is the positioning of the athlete. If a competitor is throwing a hammer in the Scottish games, they have to keep their feet rooted to one spot at all times. They are not allowed to turn their bodies in the fashion of the Olympics, rather they must orbit the weight around themselves with their back to the field.

Record Holder

The current record holder for Hammer is Daniel McKim, at the 2014 Utah Highland Games. He threw an incredible 132' 10-1/4" in the Heavy Hammer and 157' 7-1/4" in the 16lb light hammer.

Stone Put: Open and Braemar

There are two different kinds of stone-throwing events, these events usually consist of the use of a smooth river stone and the difference in these two events is that of the stone's weight and the technique that may be used to throw the stone. These events are called the Open Stone and the Braemar Stone.

The How

The Braemar event requires competitors to throw a heavier stone which must be thrown from a stationary position, with no forward movement of the feet. The stone that is thrown by men usually weighs somewhere between 20 to 26 pounds, while the stone thrown by women can weigh 13 to 18 pounds.

In contrast, the Open Stone competition allows competitors to throw a lighter stone. For men, the weight requirement is between 16 and 22 pounds, while females can throw a stone that weighs between 8 to 12 pounds.

Additionally, men and women do *not* have to stay rooted in one spot while they're throwing the stone. Many athletes either *spin* before they throw the stone or *glide.* These are two different techniques that are employed by competitors to further the distance of their throw. Both of these techniques tend to look a bit like a hop and a shuffle.

Record Holders

Record holder for the women's class Open Stone was in 2000 by Shannon Hartnett at Callander Scotland, she threw a massive 44' 2" with a 14lb stone.

The lightweight men Braemar record was thrown in 2012 at Las Vegas NV, by Jacob Nicol, with 36' 5" on a 22lb stone

Weight Contests

Weight Over the Bar (WOB)

In this event, a weight that is attached to a handle is thrown above a bar for height. The starting height of this bar is set beforehand by the rules and regulations set out for the game. Participants are only allowed to use *one hand* to throw the weight over the bar. The weights are 56lbs for men, 42lbs for Masters men and 28lbs for women. The handle can sometimes vary in shape, too. Either round, triangular or D-ring.

Record Holder

In 2010 Ray Oster broke the Masters 65+ Men's record at 10' with the 56lb WOB!

Weight for Distance (LWFD/HWFD)

The regulations in weight for the Weight for Distance event are the same as the Weight Over the Bar contest. But the combination of handle-and-weight can't be more than 18" in length, whereas the WOB handle is directly linked to the weight. Additionally, weight for distance includes both a heavy and light throw. Men can throw a 28-pound weight and a 56-pound weight, while women throw either a 14-pound weight or a 28-pound weight.

In the case this competition has a Master Class, and then the weight for that competition will be 42 pounds for the heavy weight for distance. Technique for the throw varies; most competitors opt for a one or two spin throw. Timing, grip, balance, strength, speed and power all play a major role in these events

Record Holders

The LWFD Amateur record was set in Anne Arundel County MD in 2006 by Eric Frasure with 91' 9". He also holds the world's North American HWFD record at 49' 10" in Portland OR, 2008, and the Amateur in Huntersville NC, 2005 at 49' 8"

Sheaf toss

The sheaf is a burlap bag filled with bailing twine. A pitchfork, usually a traditional two or three tine fork is required to toss the sheaf into the air and over a cross bar for height.

The sheaf toss is a North American addition, it is argued exactly how it originated. However, it is fairly believable to think it came from harvesting and throwing bales of wheat and straw into wagons or lofts. However, you may rarely if ever see this event outside of the US.

The sheaf typically weighs 12-13 lbs. for women and 16-20 lbs. for men. The starting height of the bar is agreed upon by the athletes. Athletes may wait until the bar reaches the height that they wish to enter the event at.

Record Holder

The Canadian record holder is Jason Johnston, who threw a 20lb sheaf 34" 1" at Selkirk, Manitoba in 2012.

Other Events

Tug-O-War

Tug-O-War is one of the most recognizable games in the world. It's a game that needs no introduction and can be played by anyone to pass their time. One of the reasons behind the game's popularity is that Tug-O-War is one of the oldest games in the history of humanity. It dates back to 500 B.C. and was also played in ancient Greece and China. It has been a popular game throughout the ages, and up until the 1920s, it was a part of the Olympics, too.

This game was and still is the perfect blend of brute strength, attitude, and technique. As much as people would like to suggest that the game is only about strength – it's not. It is only because of its wide appeal that the game is now played all across the world, rather than just at the Scottish Highland Games.

Running/athletics
It is generally agreed that the first official recorded games was with King Malcolm in 1040AD   . Malcolm needed a courier, and he arranged a foot race to determine someone worthy of the post. Since then, foot and hill racing and other such athletic events are often within the games.

Maide Leisg/Back hold Wrestling

Maide Leisg (Lazy Stick) is a version of MAS wrestling, both competitors sit on the ground with a toe board between them at their feet. Each grasp a stick over the board and pull against each other, in an attempt to pull their opponent over the board or win the stick. Back hold wrestling is competitors beginning in a form of clinch the objective being to floor the opponent.

Highlander
Many events have become a hybrid of strongman, these events combine both Highland Games and some strongman events such as atlas stones, farmers work, keg toss etc. These competitions have come to be known as Highlander events.

Highland Dance/Piping
The Highland Games nowadays, is always a celebration as much as it is a competition. Games will be held at

Celtic festivals all over the world, where we celebrate our Celtic heritage. Often there will be pipers, traditional dancers, swordsmen/historians, bakers and a variety of market sellers, from kilts to bagpipes!

Games Day Terminology, Etiquette and Overview

There's a lot that goes on at the Highland Games. Still with me? Great! Let's talk about some common terminology, etiquette and the Games day overview.

Terminology

The Trig

Let's start with "What's a trig?" Basically, the trig a part of the throwing area or zone – This is where you start for all spins, glides and throws for the weights for distance, hammer and stones. The majority of the time in the United States, we'll see the "Box." Which measures up 4'6" wide and 9' long (7' 6" for the Open Stone). In the stone and weight events, you must start with at least one foot inside the box. For it to be counted as a *legal* throw, you must also complete the throw with at least one foot inside of the box. Both feet must always remain behind the wooden block at the front of the box.

The other form of a box, more often seen in Scotland and throughout Europe, is what is a "Winged Trig," though it has been making its way into some U.S. games. In many people's opinions, the winged trig is seen as more thrower friendly, as it is much easier to judge and there's a little more room in width for the thrower. However, differing from the trig, the athlete must begin with both feet in the box and finish with both feet in the box. The measurements remain the same of 7 '6'' and 9' in length, however the width is at 6' 9'', due to 45-degree angles from either side of the trig leading to the box.

Hammer Cage

Wondering what a hammer cage is? Picture this: Chain link fencing, set up behind the box, to hopefully stop a runaway hammer!

Standards

Standards is another name for the height rig for WOB and Sheaf. See that piece of equipment in the image below? That's a weight being thrown over the bar (Weight Over Bar) using the Standards.

Athletic Director (AD)

The Athletic Director (AD), is THE GUY. They spend so much of their free time volunteering organizing and running these Games/events, it is a "Labor of Love" as quoted by my friend and Athletic Director of the Covenanter Games in Pennsylvania.

The major roles of the AD include:

- Providing a safe field for both athletes and spectators
- Facilitate Classes of Athlete, whether it's Pro's, amateurs, women or Master's. Known as Flights - They acquire the equipment, and implements needed for the event, to include extras in case of damages

(which is definitely a thing).

- Acquiring and organizing the judges, head judge, scorekeepers, announcer and ensuring a set of rules for both judges and athletes to compete under.
- Working with the festival host/field owner to ensure a fun and safe day.
- Acquiring some kind of award or certificate for the winners and ensuring all scores get uploaded into the databases correctly.

I'll say this, the athletics directors really show their passion every single time when it comes to running these events for everybody. For example, Jason and Kirstie Corder went the extra mile organizing the 7th annual running of the Covenanter Games in PA, their first event on the East Coast, providing goodie bags for each athlete, designing t-shirts and pins, creating an awesome logo, lunch and even a wee' dram to toast a successful day. Their layout of the field, extra challenge events and running of the day was one of the most enjoyable Games experiences I have had so far.

Having run various games on the West Coast, they truly showed how amazing an event could be.

Most of the time the Games have little to no budget and the AD's will pay for items out of their own pockets to ensure success and a great day. They all deserve our respect and always our gratitude.

Judges
As with any sport, what the judge says goes. Sure, it's ok to protest a decision if warranted. Just be sure to do it in a respectful manner, these people are volunteering their time to be there and to help make it a fair, fun and competitive environment for everyone.

Shag
So, the first time I heard this I thought everyone was

just making a dirty joke. I'm British, sorry haha! What it actually means is "Pick up the weights" during game day. For all of the distance events you'd usually shag the weight for two throwers ahead. For example, all of the athletes stand in the field near the "impact area" waiting their turn to shag and then throw. Once the weight has landed on your shag, you retrieve the weight and take it to the trig for the thrower ahead of you, this puts you "On Deck" for your throw.

On Caber, the rule is throw, shag, shag. The caber always requires a two person carry. For the first shag, you will "walk it up" and on the second shag, you will support the next "walker " and assist in carry. During height events, WOB and Sheaf, you simply shag your own weight by returning it under the bar for the next thrower.

Pro tip: Never drop the weights in the throwing area, as causing unnecessary holes in the earth is not fair to your fellow competitors.

Highland Games Etiquette

Borrowing
Athletes are very friendly and accommodating people; it's one of the things I love the most about this community. That being said, you must be sure to reciprocate that same level of respect. It's always understandable to have forgotten something: tacky, chalk, tape etc. There's always plenty to go around, you just don't want to be "that guy" who never has anything. Same goes for Sheaf forks, again; if you are new, athletes would be happy to lend their forks. There's a bit of pride in an athlete's fork and many have been customized to create a very personal implement. However, once someone lends you a fork, they are trusting you to treat it with absolute respect. *Never put the points into the ground, or throw someone else's fork in anger, you'll find yourself never being lent anything again.*

Be respectful and appreciative

The Highland Games community has some of the most respectful and humble people I've ever met. However, it is still important to remember, or be reminded of a couple things, such as:

- The game day implements are community ones. Everyone is throwing them so, treat them with respect, give it a wipe off before handing it to the next thrower. Don't do anything that will cause unnecessary damage etc.
- Clean up behind yourself, pick up your trash and don't be a slob. These events are on private land, and we want to be invited back.
- There's so much time spent organizing and developing these events, awards are often homemade. It's the passion for our community that drives this and keeps it going. Don't forget to thank them for what they do.
- The Crowd. Another important one not to forget. The crowd has, the majority of the time, paid to be there. They want to see you, as an athlete, perform. These are also family events. So, showing good sportsmanship is paramount to set the example, even cussing (I try not to, but occasionally I'll let slip - I'm sorry!). Also, if someone in the crowd takes more interest, welcome them! Again, set the example and be a steward to our community.

Must Haves

What should you take with you for a successful day? Here are some of the must have items for the Games:

- Your A Game! Attitude is everything. Compete, entertain and help your fellow athletes.
- Kilt, it's literally a rule! However, wearing a kilt is a must have experience for everyone. I'll cover how and where to buy kilts in a later chapter.
- Shoes. Something with a bit of grip, not too aggressive

and something that you don't mind getting muddy. Personally, I wear Saucony track spikes. I got mine for under $30 from Eastbay.com and love that they fit nice and tight, so no slippage. The great thing about a track spike, is you've plenty of grip in the ball of your foot, but not too much that it slows you down. I started with a Rugby boot, and ended up breaking them my first games, just way too much grip. Many athletes also carry "murder Boots" or "blades", these scary looking footwears are used during the hammer throw.

- Sheaf fork. A two, or three tine fork depending on what the event allows.
- Towel, dry socks and shirt. I'm sure the reasons are obvious, something to change into, dry off and get a little more comfortable after a whole day.
- Tacky/Tape - There's usually plenty to go around, but refer back to borrowing... Don't be the guy that never has any.
- Wrists wraps/Weight Belt (neoprene or soft leather). A lot of throwers will use wraps during stones, and belts for WOB or sheaf. There's no need for the thick lever belts, just something to make you feel a little better.
- Sunscreen/Sunhat. You're going to be out all day, literally, for these events. Trust me, you're going to need it.
- Hoodie/wet weather jacket. Again, the reasons should be obvious.
- Hand cleaner and multi tool. Tacky is pine tar or sap, it gets everywhere! I carry a fast orange, pumice hand cleaner, and my handy dandy towel. Good to go. Your multi tool is also there for a number of quick field jobs, should they arise.
- Canopy. This is basically your dressing room. It also keeps you out of the sun or rain.
- Lastly, I'll add that you're going to need a box or at

least a big bag to carry everything.
- Fuel -Water, water, water! Lots of it.
- Gatorade/Electrolyte powder. This helps keep you hydrated during that long day in the sun.
- Protein bars/Jerky/Bananas. Keeps you fueled throughout the day. Bananas have tons of potassium to stave off cramps, but if you're hydrated that should be a non-issue!

And if this is your first ever game, don't worry about going out and spending money on all this, just show up and people will welcome you and lend you what you need to get you through the day. No sense in wasting cash if you decide it's not for you, but at least you gave it a go right?!

Game Day Overview
So, how does the day roll?

The field is normally set up the day prior to the event with height rigs, trigs and hammer cages. Games day arrival is usually pretty early in the morning; Athletes will arrive any time before 0700. They're quick to set up their spaces and canopies and greet each other. It really does give you that sense of what it may have been like hundreds of years ago when these warrior clans would gather.

Soon thereafter, the AD is going to give their brief on how the day will run, who the judge is for each class as well as taking roll call of what athletes are on the field and advising of any other pertinent information.

Then it begins! Somewhere between 0900 and 1000, the Games will officially begin - by which event will depend on what class you're in. For me, it's been the norm to get stones, hammers and weights for distance done before lunch. That's 6 of the 9 events! Caber is always a crowd pleaser, so that tends to be done at peak festival attendance, which is right after lunch.

With that being said, be careful not to eat too big or heavy a meal! I made this mistake once and once only haha.

That'll leave WOB and sheaf for the end of day events. They normally take a while because each athlete has three attempts *per height*. So, athletes will grab their chairs from their respective areas and hangout around the standards.

And there you go... Around 4:30pm/5pm the Games are over, scores are collected, and awards are given. Then we celebrate! There is very much a work hard, play harder mentality here. You'll love it!

Governing Bodies

This is going to be more focused on the US, as that's where I'm based, and I honestly just don't know what all the governing bodies are around the world. Having said that. It may seem weird to a newcomer to think we have multiple governing bodies for just one sport.

There are two sides to this proverbial fence. On the one side, many think the Highland Games should be covered by just one governing body with standardized weights and rules and I understand this concept for simplicity's sake.

However, on the other side of this opinion is the historical aspect. Years ago, Clan gatherings would have people come together from all over the Highlands and whichever Clan or area in which you gathered, that Clan was the governing body. While the general concept of the games is the same more or less everywhere, much like a caber or stone, you can't tell it to grow or form to a certain specification. So attending one Clan's gathering you will have certain stone's and cabers. The next Clan will have one's that may differ slightly in size, length, weight or shape.

The Scottish Highland Games Association (SHGA)
Established in 1947 and recognized by the United

Kingdom and Scottish Governments as the official Highland Games governing body. The SHGA leads where the rest of the world follows. The SHGA has standardized much of the Games such as weights, classes etc. They are also the ones that made the wearing of a Kilt an official rule to compete in order to further promote culture. http://www.shga.co.uk/

International Highland Games Federation (IHGF)

Founded in 2001 in the USA by Francis Brebner. Francis holds multiple World Champion titles and various World Records in the Highland Games. The IHGF is probably one of the largest governing bodies outside of Scotland, with twenty-three affiliated countries to date, throughout Europe including many Games in the Western United States. https://internationalhighlandgamesfederation.com/

Scottish Masters Athletics International (SMAI)

The exclusive sanctioning body for the Masters World Championships, the annual amateur competition for over 40 Heavy Athletes. https://scottishmasters.org/

Southeastern Highland Athletics Group (SHAG)

Founded by and ran by current and former Athletes. SHAG governs and organizes games thorough FL, TN, GA, SC, NC and southern VA. http://www.throwshagshag.org/

MID-Atlantic Scottish Athletics (MASA)

Founded in 1999, MASA continues to organize events and games in MD, PA, WV, KY, Northern VA and OH. http://www.heavyevents.com/

Rocky Mountain Scottish Athletics (RMSA)

As the name suggests, the RMSA is headed in Colorado and covers the Mid-Western states such as, CO, WY and NM

North American Scottish Games Athletics (NASGA)

NAGA is not a governing body in the sense of control

and organization of games, it is used as a database for all athlete scores and rankings throughout the US. It was founded in 1976 by father and son duo Jim and Kurt Pauli. http://www.nasgaweb.com/about.asp

How to Get Started in the Highland Games

Getting started in the Highland Games is actually very easy! Find a Games, contact the organizer, show up and throw!

For me, I started without knowing anyone in the community. The Highland Games was something that I had wanted to participate in for a long time. Out of fear of embarrassment, lack of experience and not knowing anyone, I dragged my feet. It's funny, because as I write this, a friend of mine is traveling to the Iron Thistle Scottish Festival in OK and she had ordered some clothes from Spanx and was super excited about the delivery. The package arrived just in time for her to leave, and inside the box was written; "The biggest risk in life is not risking". Which in my case at the time, was absolutely true. I didn't risk or choose action. Instead, my wife saw a sponsored post for The Covenanter Games in Quarryville, PA come across her Newsfeed on Facebook. She emailed the organizer and signed me up!

The day of the Games, she got me packed up and pushed me to just do it. I will be forever grateful to her for pushing me. At Covenanter I was greeted, welcomed, coached and had one of the best competition days in my life. I did fall down, but only once and it was a pretty good fall, too. I learned the importance of letting go of the Hammer. It was this very day that I fell in love with this sport. Since then I have tried to attend every Highland Games event that I can along the East Coast, with plans to travel farther and more often in the next season.

The community, the support, the event itself, the history,

the kilts! It is all absolutely amazing.

Social media has now brought us all so much closer together, and that in turn has made it fairly simple to get started.

The Covenanter Game, my first ever Highland Games event, was just a small local Games at the time. So, signing up was just that simple, my wife emailed the organizer and we just showed up on Game day. Most other Highland Games are held within a Scottish/Celtic Festival and the Games themselves are organized by one of the Governing bodies.

By searching for Scottish/Highland/Celtic Festivals, you will be pleasantly surprised by just how many and how often these festivals are held in the US. From there you will find if the respective festival also hosts a Games and you can go from there. Another option to finding events in your area is to search for the term "Highland Games" itself. Bear in mind that many Heavy Athletics Athletes also have their own throwing clubs and Clans for example.

Clan Adrenalin in the Virginia area is headed by one of the kindest and most passionate men I've met in this sport.

Sometimes even entire states will have a group, such as Utah Heavy Athletics, or the Old Bay Highlanders in MD. Just talk to an athlete!

The best advice on getting started that I can give you is this: Go to an event or message one of these groups and *just talk to one of those brutes* in a kilt. Trust me, the community is extremely friendly and any one of the men or women athletes would be happy to point you in the right direction. It's really just that simple.

Pro Tip: If you find a Games you'd like to participate in, find out what day registration will open and sign up ASAP. Spots tend to fill up fast as the sport is quite a popular one and space is limited.

Clans

A large part of the Highland Games culture consists of the clans. From colorful tartans all around to educational booths, the Highland Games and Celtic festivals are always sure to have something for everyone. There are a number of ways you can find your clan, but perhaps the easiest is to check this website:

https://www.scotclans.com/scottish-clans/whats-my-clan/

Here's the thing, if it works for you then great. You'll need to bring your A game to really find your clan there. As in, I hope you've researched your family tree and found your Scottish roots, because that's the name you should query the website for. More often than not, no results will return without it.

Here's another one that's about on par with the previous website:

https://clan.com/families

Finding your clan is the equivalent of a cultural scavenger hunt.

Don't lose faith. I believe in you! Finding your clan can help you find a piece of yourself. Celebrate your Scottish heritage by proudly displaying your crest and tartan - and what better place to do that than a Celtic festival and Highland Games, where you're sure to meet some like-minded individuals, new friends and a few extremely distant (to the max) relatives!

This next link is an absolute treasure trove to help get in touch with your Scottish roots as it is the home to thousands of Scottish records, dating all the way back to the 1500's.

https://www.scotlandspeople.gov.uk/

Famous Clans

There are loads of clans out there. Here's a few of the more famous clans to get you started.

- Bruce (think Robert the Bruce)
- Baird
- Cameron
- Douglas (a powerful clan in Scotland)
- Erskine
- Fraser (any Outlander fans out there?!)
- Grant
- Gordon
- McKenzie (that's my clan!!)
- Munro
- Robertson

Don't forget to also checkout the map at the front of this book as well to see not only what some of the other clans were, but where they were from.

Kilts

If you haven't already figured it out, kilts are a HUGE part of the Scottish culture and the Highland Games. In this chapter, we'll walk you through how to find your clan's tartan, where to buy your kilt from, what's under the kilt along with touching on a few accessories to pair with your kilt - such as the sgian dubh and sporran.

How to Choose a Tartan

Tartan is a cloth pattern made up of squares in alternating colors. You may know it better by another term: *plaid*.

For centuries, the tartan remained an essential part of the everyday garb of Highlanders. While tartan was also worn in other parts of Scotland, it was in the Highlands that its advancement sustained, and thus it became tantamount with the symbol of clan kinship.

The tartan would go on to become outlawed in 1746 with the proscription Act. This would last approximately 40 years until it was repealed in 1782.

The Great Tartan Revival began in 1822, George IV visited Edinburgh. Not only was he the first King to visit Scotland in 150 years, but he also came in full Highland

Dress! At the event the Scots were encouraged to attend in their respective tartans. Unfortunately, many of the original Tartan patterns had been lost since Culloden and it was necessary for some redesigning by the kilt makers of the time. Tartans are nowadays officially registered with respective Clans or family names and organizations.

Women would also (and still do!) wear the tartan. Originally female plaid was known as an "earasaid." The earasaid would be worn slightly differently than the plaid of a kilt, allowing for a hood.

So, if you are confused about which tartan you should wear, for instance, at the Highland Games, or any occasion for that matter, relax and read on and choose the most appropriate tartan for yourself.

Which Tartan Should You Wear?

Simply put, wear whichever tartans strike your fancy. While there is a traditional aspect to family heritage on which Tartan you have the "right" to wear, nobody is ever going to tell you that you can't, as the wearing and promotion of highland dress is strongly encouraged.

With over two thousand tartans, picking the "right" tartan for yourself can be quite a challenging task. Searching for Irish and Scottish tartans by surname might help taper the quantity of tartans to choose from, but then you will have to deal with other considerations such as the type of tartan, its weight, the mill that weaves it, the type of material, etc.

So, before we begin, I want to dissuade the notion that there's a single "appropriate" tartan for you. There are several tartans that you can wear proudly that reflect your identity and or heritage.

Types of Tartans

Types of tartans are divided into three main categories: region, clan, and organization.

- *Clan tartans* – They are the most primeval type of tartan and are associated with a family or clan. Only Welsh and Scottish tartans are associated with clan names, whereas the Irish have regionally associated tartans.
- *Organizational tartans* – These tartans are worn by individuals who belong to a certain organization. These tartans are most commonly associated with musical or military groups.
- *Regional tartans* – As mentioned earlier, the Irish tartans are associated with the geographic counties where the clan/family lived rather than with a specific name. Common last names are associated with multiple Irish counties, while less common last names are only associated with a single Irish county.

Delving deeper on the subject each Tartan, may have multiple versions;

- Dress Tartan - Usually, lighter colors with white backgrounds.
- Mourning Tartans - generally blacks and whites in the pattern
- Hunting Tartan - Subdued colors, worn for sport. Especially if that Clans tartan was so vibrant in color making it useless to hunt.
- Chief's Tartan - For personal use of the Clan Chieftain

The only tartan considered "off limits" is the Royal Family's Balmoral Tartan, designed by HRH Prince Albert in 1857. Tradition dictates this may only be worn by the Royal Family, or at the permission of Her Majesty the Queen. Currently, the only Non-Royal permitted to wear the Balmoral Tartan is the Royal Piper to the Sovereign.

Weight, Prices and Other Tedium of Tartans

The kilt is made up of a length of fabric resulting in an inside and outside apron with buckle closures (and fringe if traditional) with a series of folds (pleats) at the back.

- *Tartan price* – The cost of a wool kilt is determined by the mill that makes the kilt, its weight, and how rare the tartan weave is. Rare tartans are more expensive because they are typically woven by only one mill. In contrast, common tartans are less expensive thanks to high competition.
- *Tartan weight* – The typical weight for a kilt is sixteen ounces. Considering all the pleating in a kilt, sixteen-ounce fabric produces a hefty garment that is ideal for the Highlands of Scotland. But kilt connoisseurs seeking more of a breeze favor the thirteen-ounce fabric. Nonetheless, I discourage buying kilts with fabric that weighs less than thirteen-ounce.
- *Yardage* - Kilts are generally sold in 5, 8 even 9 yards, what that means is the total length of material used to make the finished kilt. From the front, both of these look the same, the difference is at the back with the amount and width of pleats that are put into the Kilt. The major differences will be the weight and cost. Nobody's checking whether you have an 8 or a 5 yard. However, my opinion would be, don't do less than 5 yards, as the kilt may have too few pleats at the back from an aesthetics point of view.
- *Pleat to Sett or Stripe?* - The sett is basically the Tartan pattern. So, pleating to the Sett would mean that the same pattern repeats throughout the kilt. Pleating to the stripe is where each pleat is slightly offset to wear the Plaid repeats (The Stripe), this results in a very bold striped pattern at the back, with the regular plaid at the apron.

So, Which Tartan Should You Wear?

Honestly, buy a tartan that you'll wear. Whether it is the

tartan that has your favorite color combo, looks best on you, or the tartan associated with your clan; Get a tartan in which you'll receive the most enjoyment. Having said that. It's not necessary to choose a Tartan at all, many kilts today are made in various materials and of differing designs. You have the ability to choose from plain colors, camouflage and all types of pattern.

Where to Buy a Kilt?

In the 1800s, if you sought to buy a kilt in Scotland, you'd directly head to your local kilt maker. Unfortunately, it's very rare for an individual to have a "local kilt maker in today's time." That's why "where to buy a kilt?" is one of the most searched questions regarding kilts.

The short answer to this question is: *you can buy a kilt in-person at a festival/local shop or online.*

However, in order to answer where to buy. We must first look at; How to buy a Kilt?

You need to start by looking at the type of kilt you want, what will you be using it for?

- Formal occasion?
- Sporting event?
- Everyday wear?

There's an abundance of material and patterns out there nowadays, so there is something for everybody. Personally, I currently own two kilts, both in my Clan Tartan (Mckenzie). One is acrylic for sport and everyday use because it's very easy to clean and care for, the other is wool for formal wear. Both Kilts however are very traditional in look; leather buckles, fringe, lots of pleats (to the sett). I love them!

The other aspect to look at is the price. Now a kilt can run you anywhere from $60 to $600, depending where and what you buy. Many people own just one kilt or rent because of this and only wear on very formal occasions.

Luckily, modern age and access have made this traditional dress so much more accessible to everyone and kilts can be enjoyed from sporting events, concerts, hunting, hiking and beyond!

Measuring for your kilt is probably the most important part in this process, as there is a right and wrong way in kilt wear for men. Too short and it's essentially a miniskirt, too long and you'll look like you're in a dress. Fortunately for the ladies, there are no rules, go nuts!

Traditional kilt wear should be around the True Waist (at the navel) and the length should come to the middle of your knee cap.

To measure for this, you'll need a tailors tape, and you will take the waist measurement all the way around your true waist, keeping the tap level and crossing the navel. It's important to understand that the folds which form the pleat in the kilt create a lot of material around its waist. So, you will need to add at least 2 inches to compensate for the extra material.

The second measurement will go from about 4 inches to either side of your navel, and straight down to the center of your knee cap. It's important to stand straight here, so you might need a buddy.

Now, these are the simplest of measurements that will get you what you need from any reputable online kilt shop.

In person would be the best experience when it comes to buying a kilt, as the craftsmen will be able to ensure a true fit at the store. Unfortunately, there aren't many local kiltmakers down the road. Spring City, PA is the home of USA Kilts. If you're looking for the in-person experience, I highly recommend visiting them. The owners are masters of their craft and have a true passion for kilts and Celtic heritage. They also have a YouTube channel dedicated to answering many kilted questions. Check them out! https://www.usakilts.com/

Buying online is most likely the viable option for most of us. (It was for me). However, finding a quality and reputable kilt seller online can be difficult.

SportKilt is quite a popular brand and they make durable and lightweight kilts intended for, you guessed it. Sport, and any occasion honestly, they are well made from synthetic materials and easy to care for. https://sportkilt. com/

My personal favorite is UT Kilts. There are a few reasons for my opinion. First off, I love the care and attention the owner gives every single one of his customers.

UT Kilts has the most variety. There is a kilt for everybody, every occasion and everyone is made with such incredible care and attention, and if it doesn't fit, he has a "Fit Guarantee" that will ensure your satisfaction.

Brice Lythgoe, started UT Kilts after instead of buying his first kilt, Made it! Brice's passion for kilt making and wanting everybody to be able to afford the luxury of wearing a kilt outweigh the opportunity to just "do it for the money", now after almost 10 years of business, he has never raised his prices. Making his wool, that's right! (I have one) Wool kilts, that are some of the most affordable quality kilts I have seen. UT Kilts, also has a YouTube channel that covers many "How Tos" of kilt wearing. https://www.utkilts.com/

What's Under the Kilt?
Wouldn't you like to know…

I think it's safe to assume that many automatically think that when a man is wearing a kilt, he's gone commando, airing out his bits.

How's the breeze down there?

But seriously, what's worn under the kilt?

Scottish Tradition

Where would we be if not for traditions?! Historians believe the tradition of wearing no undergarments under a kilt can be traced back to Scottish military regiments. It's rumored that in the 18th century the Scottish military dress code prescribed kilts but did not specify one way or the other regarding undergarments. Now, for those familiar with the Scottish, you can probably understand the accuracy of the sentiment here... Those very same Scottish troops took that as a challenge, going without undergarments. And it was through this oversight/challenge that the tradition of going "Regimental" under the kilt was born.

This tradition was not for everyone when wearing a kilt and there are those on both sides of the garment covered fence. Which is absolutely fine! Whose business is it to be an underwear checker anyway? Both, the Scottish Board of Highland Dancing and as a ruling within the Highland Games has in fact, made it a part of the dress code that anyone competing while wearing a kilt must also be wearing undergarments.

Sgian Dubh

Ah, my friend, the piece de resistance to wearing a kilt is the sgian dubh (pronounced: sken-DOO). A true Scotsman is never without it. It is a small dagger which is worn with a kilt.

Sgian dubh, translated from Gaelic, means "black dagger" or "black knife". It is said that the name derives from the fact that the blade was initially worn and concealed, steeped in secrecy, with it's dark past.

The sgian dubh were wildly popular during the 17th and 18th centuries. It was originally worn on the upper body, under the armpit and has since evolved to be worn in the Kilt sock, held in place with garters. Residing in a scabbard, the blade is generally under inches in length and is most often made from steel.

Today, the sgian dubh is worn partially concealed in the kilt hose as part of the full Highland dress. It is typically worn on your dominant hand's side - allowing quick access to the blade... just in case.

The mount of the sgian dubh was typically engraved with the family crest or even coat of arms to show their status and their identity. Celtic knotwork was also a favored design which would be engraved on quite a few sgian dubhs.

While initially used for survival, today the sgian dubh is more decorative and used for ceremonial purposes.

Sporran

The Sporran is an essential part of a full Highland Dress. It is a pouch, made from leather or fur and worn to the front of the wearer on a leather strap and chain.

It's important to note that it's a good idea to take it off if you plan to participate in the Highland Games (guys, you'll regret it).

Much like the tartan, the sporran also comes in a variety of options;

- **Day Sporran** - Intended for everyday use and made entirely of leather, often with Celtic Knotwork or design embossed into the leather
- **Dress Sporran** - A more ornate and larger version of the day sporran. Often with a fur face with fur or hair tassels, the cantle is often Stirling or silver plated with intricate etchings of Celtic knotwork.
- **Horsehair Sporran** - Commonly associated with Regimental dress. This is one of the biggest and most ornate of the sporrans, with a very formal style. Traditionally, the hair will extend to just below the hem of the kilt with black horsehair tassels on a white hair background and carved pewter, or silver cantle

with regimental crest.

- **Mask Sporran** - Made from the hide of a badger, fox coyote or other small animal. The head of the animal typically forms the front flap of the pouch with the rest of the hide forming the actual pouch.
- **Ysgrepan** - The Welsh equivalent to the Scottish Sporran. (Pronounced: Es - gre - pan). Made from Welsh horsehair and goatskin, with a large leather flap often embossed with the Welsh Dragon.

Proper wear of the sporran, should be to the front of the kilt , to the side if dancing, or if whatever you're doing is causing it to swing a lot, I'm sure you can guess why. Lastly, the sporran shouldn't hang too low, about 4-5 inches, or a hands breadth from the top of the kilt.

Kilt Pin

The kilt pin is another decorative, yet essential piece to full dress. It is only meant to go through the outer apron of the kilt. It's function, to weigh the apron down in windy weather avoiding any unpleasantries. For this reason, pins are generally made from metal and come in a huge variety from clan and family crests, to handmade pieces.

12-Week Training Log
(4 per week)

Use this log to record your
Highland Games training, PRs,
goals, notes, etc.

How to use the training log

I have tried to set this up as user friendly as possible. For me I think it works pretty well, and I'm sure for new thrower development, this'll get you on the right track.

Events Table

Here is listed all the events you will see at the games throughout the States. For a training day, I will only work on 3 events at a time mixing up heavy and light events. So, if I am training HWFD, I will pair that with Light Hammer and one of the height events. Also, I will always start a session with a warmup on open stone because I am working on the spin and find it is low impact enough to not do me an injury. You can use this table to track your scores and PR's at an actual Games also.

For each practice, you want to build up to the full throw. For example, Light Hammer. Start with 1 wind for 5 reps, 2 winds for 10 reps and finish with 5 reps of full 3 wind and throws. These are the scores you measure. I like doing it this way, because through the fatigue of a long session I feel like I show the most progress at the next Games. Also, measuring the 5 best and 5 worst throws, gives me good numbers to work on my Grid/Consistency portion.

Drills

Depending on what your focus is on a given training day, writing my drills out helps me keep focus on what I am working on.

Grid/Consistency

I like using this method a whole lot. There are a lot of throwers out there who can throw big numbers on occasion, but lack in consistency. That is where this table comes in. You can either take your worst/best of 5's from above or go for your PR and around 80% of it.

Whichever works for you, measure out both distances and mark with a cone, flag, or something you don't mind getting smashed and throw into that Grid. Reps is up to you, go for as many reps as possible and consistently hit that grid. As you get better and your worst of best of distance get closer together, your throwing box will get smaller and smaller, improving accuracy and your throw overall.

I've filled an example sheet on the next page for you. Enjoy your training and the process that comes with it. Remember, throw farther, suck less!

Height			
Braemar			
Open			
LWFD			
HWFD	track you PR here		
L Hammer	Example - 87' 2"	83' 6"	79' 9"
H Hammer			
WOB			
Sheaf	Circle the throws for the training days concentration		
Caber (Turn)	Y/N	Y/N	Y/N

Drills ran today
(e.g. battle drill/pick and carry)

Bottle Drill - 10 mins as warm up	
Line Drill - 5 mins	
Caber - Pick and Carry	

Grid Consistency/Volume Training

Event	Current PR	80%	# of Reps
L Hammer	87" 2"	69' 7"	8 Full throws

Week 1 - 1

Events	Distance/ Height	Best of 5	Worst of 5
Braemar			
Open			
LWFD			
HFWD			
L Hammer			
H Hammer			
WOB			
Shaef			
Caber (Turn)			

Drills ran today
(e.g. battle drill/pick and carry)

_____

_____

_____

_____

Grid Consistency/Volume Training

Events	Current PR	80%	# of Reps

They that live longest see most

Notes: How did you feel today? (e.g. sleep, diet, etc.)

_____

_____

_____

_____

_____

Notes: How did the session go? (e.g. Improves/Goals for the next session)

_____

_____

_____

_____

Notes:

_____

_____

_____

_____

Week 1 - 2

Events	Distance/ Height	Best of 5	Worst of 5
Braemar			
Open			
LWFD			
HFWD			
L Hammer			
H Hammer			
WOB			
Shaef			
Caber (Turn)			

Drills ran today
(e.g. battle drill/pick and carry)

_____

_____

_____

_____

Grid Consistency/Volume Training

Events	Current PR	80%	# of Reps

It's a slow process
but quitting won't speed it up

———◆◇◆———

Notes: How did you feel today? (e.g. sleep, diet, etc.)

_____

_____

_____

_____

_____

Notes: How did the session go? (e.g. Improves/Goals for the next session)

_____

_____

_____

_____

Notes:

_____

_____

_____

_____

_____

Week 1 - 3

Events	Distance/Height	Best of 5	Worst of 5
Braemar			
Open			
LWFD			
HFWD			
L Hammer			
H Hammer			
WOB			
Shaef			
Caber (Turn)			

Drills ran today
(e.g. battle drill/pick and carry)

_____

_____

_____

_____

Grid Consistency/Volume Training

Events	Current PR	80%	# of Reps

Do something today that your future self will thank you for

Notes: How did you feel today? (e.g. sleep, diet, etc.)

_____

_____

_____

_____

_____

Notes: How did the session go? (e.g. Improves/Goals for the next session)

_____

_____

_____

_____

_____

Notes:

_____

_____

_____

_____

_____

Week 1 - 4

Events	Distance/ Height	Best of 5	Worst of 5
Braemar			
Open			
LWFD			
HFWD			
L Hammer			
H Hammer			
WOB			
Shaef			
Caber (Turn)			

Drills ran today
(e.g. battle drill/pick and carry)

_____

_____

_____

Grid Consistency/Volume Training

Events	Current PR	80%	# of Reps

Results happen over time, not overnight.
Work hard, stay consistent and be patient

———————◆◇◆———————

Notes: How did you feel today? (e.g. sleep, diet, etc.)

_____

_____

_____

_____

_____

Notes: How did the session go? (e.g. Improves/Goals for the next session)

_____

_____

_____

_____

Notes:

_____

_____

_____

_____

_____

Week 2 - 1

Events	Distance/ Height	Best of 5	Worst of 5
Braemar			
Open			
LWFD			
HFWD			
L Hammer			
H Hammer			
WOB			
Shaef			
Caber (Turn)			

Drills ran today
(e.g. battle drill/pick and carry)

_____

_____

_____

Grid Consistency/Volume Training

Events	Current PR	80%	# of Reps

Results happen over time, not overnight.
Work hard, stay consistent and be patient

Notes: How did you feel today? (e.g. sleep, diet, etc.)

_____

_____

_____

_____

_____

Notes: How did the session go? (e.g. Improves/Goals for the next session)

_____

_____

_____

_____

_____

Notes:

_____

_____

_____

_____

_____

Week 2 - 1

Events	Distance/ Height	Best of 5	Worst of 5
Braemar			
Open			
LWFD			
HFWD			
L Hammer			
H Hammer			
WOB			
Shaef			
Caber (Turn)			

Drills ran today
(e.g. battle drill/pick and carry)

_____

_____

_____

_____

Grid Consistency/Volume Training

Events	Current PR	80%	# of Reps

Each day is a new opportunity to improve yourself. Take it and make the most of it

Notes: How did you feel today? (e.g. sleep, diet, etc.)

_____

_____

_____

_____

_____

Notes: How did the session go? (e.g. Improves/Goals for the next session)

_____

_____

_____

_____

_____

Notes:

_____

_____

_____

_____

_____

Week 2 - 2

Events	Distance/ Height	Best of 5	Worst of 5
Braemar			
Open			
LWFD			
HFWD			
L Hammer			
H Hammer			
WOB			
Shaef			
Caber (Turn)			

Drills ran today
(e.g. battle drill/pick and carry)

_____

_____

_____

_____

Grid Consistency/Volume Training

Events	Current PR	80%	# of Reps

Just believe in yourself

Notes: How did you feel today? (e.g. sleep, diet, etc.)

_____

_____

_____

_____

_____

Notes: How did the session go? (e.g. Improves/Goals for the next session)

_____

_____

_____

_____

Notes:

_____

_____

_____

_____

Week 2 - 3

Events	Distance/ Height	Best of 5	Worst of 5
Braemar			
Open			
LWFD			
HFWD			
L Hammer			
H Hammer			
WOB			
Shaef			
Caber (Turn)			

Drills ran today
(e.g. battle drill/pick and carry)

_____

_____

_____

_____

Grid Consistency/Volume Training

Events	Current PR	80%	# of Reps

Focus on where you want to be - not where you are or where you were

———————◆◇◆———————

Notes: How did you feel today? (e.g. sleep, diet, etc.)

_____

_____

_____

_____

_____

Notes: How did the session go? (e.g. Improves/Goals for the next session)

_____

_____

_____

_____

_____

Notes:

_____

_____

_____

_____

_____

Week 2 - 4

Events	Distance/ Height	Best of 5	Worst of 5
Braemar			
Open			
LWFD			
HFWD			
L Hammer			
H Hammer			
WOB			
Shaef			
Caber (Turn)			

Drills ran today
(e.g. battle drill/pick and carry)

_____

_____

_____

Grid Consistency/Volume Training

Events	Current PR	80%	# of Reps

Don't stop until you're proud of yourself

Notes: How did you feel today? (e.g. sleep, diet, etc.)

_____

_____

_____

_____

_____

Notes: How did the session go? (e.g. Improves/Goals for the next session)

_____

_____

_____

_____

_____

Notes:

_____

_____

_____

_____

_____

Week 3 - 1

Events	Distance/ Height	Best of 5	Worst of 5
Braemar			
Open			
LWFD			
HFWD			
L Hammer			
H Hammer			
WOB			
Shaef			
Caber (Turn)			

Drills ran today
(e.g. battle drill/pick and carry)

_____

_____

_____

Grid Consistency/Volume Training

Events	Current PR	80%	# of Reps

The pain you feel today is the strength you will feel tomorrow

Notes: How did you feel today? (e.g. sleep, diet, etc.)

_____

_____

_____

_____

_____

Notes: How did the session go? (e.g. Improves/Goals for the next session)

_____

_____

_____

_____

_____

Notes:

_____

_____

_____

_____

_____

Week 3 - 2

Events	Distance/Height	Best of 5	Worst of 5
Braemar			
Open			
LWFD			
HFWD			
L Hammer			
H Hammer			
WOB			
Shaef			
Caber (Turn)			

Drills ran today
(e.g. battle drill/pick and carry)

_____

_____

_____

Grid Consistency/Volume Training

Events	Current PR	80%	# of Reps

You may not be there yet, but you're closer than you were yesterday

Notes: How did you feel today? (e.g. sleep, diet, etc.)

_____

_____

_____

_____

_____

Notes: How did the session go? (e.g. Improves/Goals for the next session)

_____

_____

_____

_____

_____

Notes:

_____

_____

_____

_____

_____

Week 3 - 3

Events	Distance/ Height	Best of 5	Worst of 5
Braemar			
Open			
LWFD			
HFWD			
L Hammer			
H Hammer			
WOB			
Shaef			
Caber (Turn)			

Drills ran today
(e.g. battle drill/pick and carry)

_____

_____

_____

_____

Grid Consistency/Volume Training

Events	Current PR	80%	# of Reps

The only bad workout is the one that didn't happen

—◆◇◆—

Notes: How did you feel today? (e.g. sleep, diet, etc.)

_____

_____

_____

_____

_____

Notes: How did the session go? (e.g. Improves/Goals for the next session)

_____

_____

_____

_____

_____

Notes:

_____

_____

_____

_____

_____

Week 3 - 4

Events	Distance/Height	Best of 5	Worst of 5
Braemar			
Open			
LWFD			
HFWD			
L Hammer			
H Hammer			
WOB			
Shaef			
Caber (Turn)			

Drills ran today
(e.g. battle drill/pick and carry)

_____

_____

_____

Grid Consistency/Volume Training

Events	Current PR	80%	# of Reps

Once you see results it becomes an addiction

Notes: How did you feel today? (e.g. sleep, diet, etc.)

_____

_____

_____

_____

_____

Notes: How did the session go? (e.g. Improves/Goals for the next session)

_____

_____

_____

_____

Notes:

_____

_____

_____

_____

Week 4 - 1

Events	Distance/ Height	Best of 5	Worst of 5
Braemar			
Open			
LWFD			
HFWD			
L Hammer			
H Hammer			
WOB			
Shaef			
Caber (Turn)			

Drills ran today
(e.g. battle drill/pick and carry)

_____

_____

_____

_____

Grid Consistency/Volume Training

Events	Current PR	80%	# of Reps

Discipline is doing what's right
even if you don't want to

◆◇◆

Notes: How did you feel today? (e.g. sleep, diet, etc.)

_____

_____

_____

_____

_____

Notes: How did the session go? (e.g. Improves/Goals for the next session)

_____

_____

_____

_____

_____

Notes:

_____

_____

_____

_____

_____

Week 4 - 2

Events	Distance/ Height	Best of 5	Worst of 5
Braemar			
Open			
LWFD			
HFWD			
L Hammer			
H Hammer			
WOB			
Shaef			
Caber (Turn)			

Drills ran today
(e.g. battle drill/pick and carry)

_____

_____

_____

_____

Grid Consistency/Volume Training

Events	Current PR	80%	# of Reps

Discipline is doing what's right
even if you don't want to

———◆◇◆———

Notes: How did you feel today? (e.g. sleep, diet, etc.)

_____

_____

_____

_____

_____

**Notes: How did the session go? (e.g. Improves/Goals
for the next session)**

_____

_____

_____

_____

Notes:

_____

_____

_____

_____

Week 4 - 2

Events	Distance/Height	Best of 5	Worst of 5
Braemar			
Open			
LWFD			
HFWD			
L Hammer			
H Hammer			
WOB			
Shaef			
Caber (Turn)			

Drills ran today
(e.g. battle drill/pick and carry)

_____

_____

_____

_____

Grid Consistency/Volume Training

Events	Current PR	80%	# of Reps

If it was easy, everybody would do it

Notes: How did you feel today? (e.g. sleep, diet, etc.)

_____

_____

_____

_____

_____

Notes: How did the session go? (e.g. Improves/Goals for the next session)

_____

_____

_____

_____

_____

Notes:

_____

_____

_____

_____

_____

Week 4 - 3

Events	Distance/Height	Best of 5	Worst of 5
Braemar			
Open			
LWFD			
HFWD			
L Hammer			
H Hammer			
WOB			
Shaef			
Caber (Turn)			

Drills ran today
(e.g. battle drill/pick and carry)

_____

_____

_____

_____

Grid Consistency/Volume Training

Events	Current PR	80%	# of Reps

Wake up. Work out. Look hot. Kick a$$

---◆◇◆---

Notes: How did you feel today? (e.g. sleep, diet, etc.)

_____

_____

_____

_____

_____

Notes: How did the session go? (e.g. Improves/Goals for the next session)

_____

_____

_____

_____

Notes:

_____

_____

_____

_____

_____

Week 4 - 4

Events	Distance/Height	Best of 5	Worst of 5
Braemar			
Open			
LWFD			
HFWD			
L Hammer			
H Hammer			
WOB			
Shaef			
Caber (Turn)			

Drills ran today
(e.g. battle drill/pick and carry)

_____

_____

_____

Grid Consistency/Volume Training

Events	Current PR	80%	# of Reps

You can feel sore tomorrow, or you can feel sorry tomorrow

—◆—◇—◆—

Notes: How did you feel today? (e.g. sleep, diet, etc.)

_____

_____

_____

_____

_____

Notes: How did the session go? (e.g. Improves/Goals for the next session)

_____

_____

_____

_____

_____

Notes:

_____

_____

_____

_____

_____

Week 5 - 1

Events	Distance/ Height	Best of 5	Worst of 5
Braemar			
Open			
LWFD			
HFWD			
L Hammer			
H Hammer			
WOB			
Shaef			
Caber (Turn)			

Drills ran today
(e.g. battle drill/pick and carry)

_____

_____

_____

_____

Grid Consistency/Volume Training

Events	Current PR	80%	# of Reps

I already know what giving up feels like.
I want to see what happens if I don't.

Notes: How did you feel today? (e.g. sleep, diet, etc.)

_____

_____

_____

_____

_____

Notes: How did the session go? (e.g. Improves/Goals
for the next session)

_____

_____

_____

_____

_____

Notes:

_____

_____

_____

_____

_____

Week 5 - 2

Events	Distance/Height	Best of 5	Worst of 5
Braemar			
Open			
LWFD			
HFWD			
L Hammer			
H Hammer			
WOB			
Shaef			
Caber (Turn)			

Drills ran today
(e.g. battle drill/pick and carry)

_____

_____

_____

_____

Grid Consistency/Volume Training

Events	Current PR	80%	# of Reps

Win that battle in your mind
and kill it in the gym

——————◆◇◆——————

Notes: How did you feel today? (e.g. sleep, diet, etc.)

_____

_____

_____

_____

_____

Notes: How did the session go? (e.g. Improves/Goals for the next session)

_____

_____

_____

_____

_____

Notes:

_____

_____

_____

_____

_____

Week 5 - 3

Events	Distance/ Height	Best of 5	Worst of 5
Braemar			
Open			
LWFD			
HFWD			
L Hammer			
H Hammer			
WOB			
Shaef			
Caber (Turn)			

Drills ran today
(e.g. battle drill/pick and carry)

_____

_____

_____

_____

Grid Consistency/Volume Training

Events	Current PR	80%	# of Reps

Do it now. "Sometime" becomes "later" which becomes "never"

Notes: How did you feel today? (e.g. sleep, diet, etc.)

_____

_____

_____

_____

_____

Notes: How did the session go? (e.g. Improves/Goals for the next session)

_____

_____

_____

_____

Notes:

_____

_____

_____

_____

_____

Week 5 - 4

Events	Distance/Height	Best of 5	Worst of 5
Braemar			
Open			
LWFD			
HFWD			
L Hammer			
H Hammer			
WOB			
Shaef			
Caber (Turn)			

Drills ran today
(e.g. battle drill/pick and carry)

_____

_____

_____

_____

Grid Consistency/Volume Training

Events	Current PR	80%	# of Reps

Beast mode: ACTIVATED

Notes: How did you feel today? (e.g. sleep, diet, etc.)

_____

_____

_____

_____

_____

**Notes: How did the session go? (e.g. Improves/Goals
for the next session)**

_____

_____

_____

_____

Notes:

_____

_____

_____

_____

Week 6 - 1

Events	Distance/ Height	Best of 5	Worst of 5
Braemar			
Open			
LWFD			
HFWD			
L Hammer			
H Hammer			
WOB			
Shaef			
Caber (Turn)			

Drills ran today
(e.g. battle drill/pick and carry)

_____

_____

_____

_____

Grid Consistency/Volume Training

Events	Current PR	80%	# of Reps

Believe you can and you're halfway there

Notes: How did you feel today? (e.g. sleep, diet, etc.)

_____

_____

_____

_____

_____

Notes: How did the session go? (e.g. Improves/Goals for the next session)

_____

_____

_____

_____

Notes:

_____

_____

_____

_____

_____

Week 6 - 2

Events	Distance/Height	Best of 5	Worst of 5
Braemar			
Open			
LWFD			
HFWD			
L Hammer			
H Hammer			
WOB			
Shaef			
Caber (Turn)			

Drills ran today
(e.g. battle drill/pick and carry)

_____

_____

_____

_____

Grid Consistency/Volume Training

Events	Current PR	80%	# of Reps

Never let weakness convince you that you don't have the strength

Notes: How did you feel today? (e.g. sleep, diet, etc.)

_____

_____

_____

_____

_____

Notes: How did the session go? (e.g. Improves/Goals for the next session)

_____

_____

_____

_____

_____

Notes:

_____

_____

_____

_____

_____

Week 6 - 3

Events	Distance/ Height	Best of 5	Worst of 5
Braemar			
Open			
LWFD			
HFWD			
L Hammer			
H Hammer			
WOB			
Shaef			
Caber (Turn)			

Drills ran today
(e.g. battle drill/pick and carry)

_____

_____

_____

_____

Grid Consistency/Volume Training

Events	Current PR	80%	# of Reps

Never let weakness convince you that you don't have the strength

Notes: How did you feel today? (e.g. sleep, diet, etc.)

_____

_____

_____

_____

_____

Notes: How did the session go? (e.g. Improves/Goals for the next session)

_____

_____

_____

_____

Notes:

_____

_____

_____

_____

_____

Week 6 - 3

Events	Distance/ Height	Best of 5	Worst of 5
Braemar			
Open			
LWFD			
HFWD			
L Hammer			
H Hammer			
WOB			
Shaef			
Caber (Turn)			

Drills ran today
(e.g. battle drill/pick and carry)

_____

_____

_____

_____

Grid Consistency/Volume Training

Events	Current PR	80%	# of Reps

Know your limits and then crush them!

Notes: How did you feel today? (e.g. sleep, diet, etc.)

_____

_____

_____

_____

_____

Notes: How did the session go? (e.g. Improves/Goals for the next session)

_____

_____

_____

_____

_____

Notes:

_____

_____

_____

_____

_____

Week 6 - 4

Events	Distance/ Height	Best of 5	Worst of 5
Braemar			
Open			
LWFD			
HFWD			
L Hammer			
H Hammer			
WOB			
Shaef			
Caber (Turn)`			

Drills ran today
(e.g. battle drill/pick and carry)

_____

_____

_____

_____

Grid Consistency/Volume Training

Events	Current PR	80%	# of Reps

You can never expect to succeed if you only put in work on the days you feel like it

Notes: How did you feel today? (e.g. sleep, diet, etc.)

_____

_____

_____

_____

_____

Notes: How did the session go? (e.g. Improves/Goals for the next session)

_____

_____

_____

_____

_____

Notes:

_____

_____

_____

_____

_____

Week 7 - 1

Events	Distance/ Height	Best of 5	Worst of 5
Braemar			
Open			
LWFD			
HFWD			
L Hammer			
H Hammer			
WOB			
Shaef			
Caber (Turn)			

Drills ran today
(e.g. battle drill/pick and carry)

_____

_____

_____

_____

Grid Consistency/Volume Training

Events	Current PR	80%	# of Reps

Be savage, not average

Notes: How did you feel today? (e.g. sleep, diet, etc.)

_____

_____

_____

_____

_____

Notes: How did the session go? (e.g. Improves/Goals for the next session)

_____

_____

_____

_____

Notes:

_____

_____

_____

_____

Week 7 - 2

Events	Distance/ Height	Best of 5	Worst of 5
Braemar			
Open			
LWFD			
HFWD			
L Hammer			
H Hammer			
WOB			
Shaef			
Caber (Turn)			

Drills ran today
(e.g. battle drill/pick and carry)

_____

_____

_____

_____

Grid Consistency/Volume Training

Events	Current PR	80%	# of Reps

One day or day one - you decide

Notes: How did you feel today? (e.g. sleep, diet, etc.)

_____

_____

_____

_____

_____

Notes: How did the session go? (e.g. Improves/Goals for the next session)

_____

_____

_____

_____

Notes:

_____

_____

_____

_____

Week 7 - 3

Events	Distance/ Height	Best of 5	Worst of 5
Braemar			
Open			
LWFD			
HFWD			
L Hammer			
H Hammer			
WOB			
Shaef			
Caber (Turn)			

Drills ran today
(e.g. battle drill/pick and carry)

_____

_____

_____

_____

Grid Consistency/Volume Training

Events	Current PR	80%	# of Reps

Nothing happens until you decide
to make it happen

Notes: How did you feel today? (e.g. sleep, diet, etc.)

_____

_____

_____

_____

_____

Notes: How did the session go? (e.g. Improves/Goals for the next session)

_____

_____

_____

_____

_____

Notes:

_____

_____

_____

_____

_____

Week 7 - 4

Events	Distance/Height	Best of 5	Worst of 5
Braemar			
Open			
LWFD			
HFWD			
L Hammer			
H Hammer			
WOB			
Shaef			
Caber (Turn)			

Drills ran today
(e.g. battle drill/pick and carry)

_____

_____

_____

_____

Grid Consistency/Volume Training

Events	Current PR	80%	# of Reps

Because easy doesn't change you

———◆◇◆———

Notes: How did you feel today? (e.g. sleep, diet, etc.)

_____

_____

_____

_____

_____

Notes: How did the session go? (e.g. Improves/Goals for the next session)

_____

_____

_____

_____

Notes:

_____

_____

_____

_____

Week 8 - 1

Events	Distance/ Height	Best of 5	Worst of 5
Braemar			
Open			
LWFD			
HFWD			
L Hammer			
H Hammer			
WOB			
Shaef			
Caber (Turn)			

Drills ran today
(e.g. battle drill/pick and carry)

_____

_____

_____

Grid Consistency/Volume Training

Events	Current PR	80%	# of Reps

Men that wear kilts never get caught with their pants down

Notes: How did you feel today? (e.g. sleep, diet, etc.)

_____

_____

_____

_____

_____

Notes: How did the session go? (e.g. Improves/Goals for the next session)

_____

_____

_____

_____

_____

Notes:

_____

_____

_____

_____

_____

Week 8 - 2

Events	Distance/ Height	Best of 5	Worst of 5
Braemar			
Open			
LWFD			
HFWD			
L Hammer			
H Hammer			
WOB			
Shaef			
Caber (Turn)			

Drills ran today
(e.g. battle drill/pick and carry)

_____

_____

_____

Grid Consistency/Volume Training

Events	Current PR	80%	# of Reps

Be of good courage

Notes: How did you feel today? (e.g. sleep, diet, etc.)

_____

_____

_____

_____

_____

Notes: How did the session go? (e.g. Improves/Goals for the next session)

_____

_____

_____

_____

_____

Notes:

_____

_____

_____

_____

_____

Week 8 - 3

Events	Distance/Height	Best of 5	Worst of 5
Braemar			
Open			
LWFD			
HFWD			
L Hammer			
H Hammer			
WOB			
Shaef			
Caber (Turn)			

Drills ran today
(e.g. battle drill/pick and carry)

_____

_____

_____

Grid Consistency/Volume Training

Events	Current PR	80%	# of Reps

Every champion was once
a contender who refused to give up

————————◆◇◆————————

Notes: How did you feel today? (e.g. sleep, diet, etc.)

_____

_____

_____

_____

_____

Notes: How did the session go? (e.g. Improves/Goals for the next session)

_____

_____

_____

_____

_____

Notes:

_____

_____

_____

_____

_____

Week 8 - 4

Events	Distance/Height	Best of 5	Worst of 5
Braemar			
Open			
LWFD			
HFWD			
L Hammer			
H Hammer			
WOB			
Shaef			
Caber (Turn)			

Drills ran today
(e.g. battle drill/pick and carry)

_____

_____

_____

_____

Grid Consistency/Volume Training

Events	Current PR	80%	# of Reps

Every champion was once
a contender who refused to give up

———————◆◇◆———————

Notes: How did you feel today? (e.g. sleep, diet, etc.)

_____

_____

_____

_____

_____

Notes: How did the session go? (e.g. Improves/Goals for the next session)

_____

_____

_____

_____

_____

Notes:

_____

_____

_____

_____

_____

Week 8 - 4

Events	Distance/ Height	Best of 5	Worst of 5
Braemar			
Open			
LWFD			
HFWD			
L Hammer			
H Hammer			
WOB			
Shaef			
Caber (Turn)			

Drills ran today
(e.g. battle drill/pick and carry)

_____

_____

_____

Grid Consistency/Volume Training

Events	Current PR	80%	# of Reps

Attack wins you games,
defense wins you titles

◆◇◆

Notes: How did you feel today? (e.g. sleep, diet, etc.)

_____

_____

_____

_____

_____

Notes: How did the session go? (e.g. Improves/Goals for the next session)

_____

_____

_____

_____

_____

Notes:

_____

_____

_____

_____

_____

Week 9 - 1

Events	Distance/Height	Best of 5	Worst of 5
Braemar			
Open			
LWFD			
HFWD			
L Hammer			
H Hammer			
WOB			
Shaef			
Caber (Turn)			

Drills ran today
(e.g. battle drill/pick and carry)

_____

_____

_____

_____

Grid Consistency/Volume Training

Events	Current PR	80%	# of Reps

12 Highlanders and a bagpipe make a rebellion (*Scottish proverb*)

Notes: How did you feel today? (e.g. sleep, diet, etc.)

_____

_____

_____

_____

_____

Notes: How did the session go? (e.g. Improves/Goals for the next session)

_____

_____

_____

_____

_____

Notes:

_____

_____

_____

_____

_____

Week 9 - 2

Events	Distance/ Height	Best of 5	Worst of 5
Braemar			
Open			
LWFD			
HFWD			
L Hammer			
H Hammer			
WOB			
Shaef			
Caber (Turn)			

Drills ran today
(e.g. battle drill/pick and carry)

_____

_____

_____

_____

Grid Consistency/Volume Training

Events	Current PR	80%	# of Reps

The castle or the kilt - that is the question

---◆◇◆---

Notes: How did you feel today? (e.g. sleep, diet, etc.)

_____

_____

_____

_____

_____

Notes: How did the session go? (e.g. Improves/Goals for the next session)

_____

_____

_____

_____

_____

Notes:

_____

_____

_____

_____

_____

Week 9 - 3

Events	Distance/ Height	Best of 5	Worst of 5
Braemar			
Open			
LWFD			
HFWD			
L Hammer			
H Hammer			
WOB			
Shaef			
Caber (Turn)			

Drills ran today
(e.g. battle drill/pick and carry)

_____

_____

_____

_____

Grid Consistency/Volume Training

Events	Current PR	80%	# of Reps

Fools look to tomorrow.
Wise men use tonight (*Scottish proverb*)

◆◇◆

Notes: How did you feel today? (e.g. sleep, diet, etc.)

_____

_____

_____

_____

_____

**Notes: How did the session go? (e.g. Improves/Goals
for the next session)**

_____

_____

_____

_____

_____

Notes:

_____

_____

_____

_____

_____

Week 9 - 4

Events	Distance/Height	Best of 5	Worst of 5
Braemar			
Open			
LWFD			
HFWD			
L Hammer			
H Hammer			
WOB			
Shaef			
Caber (Turn)			

Drills ran today
(e.g. battle drill/pick and carry)

_____

_____

_____

_____

Grid Consistency/Volume Training

Events	Current PR	80%	# of Reps

Forgive your enemy but remember the
bastard's name (*Scottish proverb*).

———◆◇◆———

Notes: How did you feel today? (e.g. sleep, diet, etc.)

_____

_____

_____

_____

_____

**Notes: How did the session go? (e.g. Improves/Goals
for the next session)**

_____

_____

_____

_____

_____

Notes:

_____

_____

_____

_____

_____

Week 10 - 1

Events	Distance/ Height	Best of 5	Worst of 5
Braemar			
Open			
LWFD			
HFWD			
L Hammer			
H Hammer			
WOB			
Shaef			
Caber (Turn)			

Drills ran today
(e.g. battle drill/pick and carry)

_____

_____

_____

_____

Grid Consistency/Volume Training

Events	Current PR	80%	# of Reps

Go ahead… I dare you to call my kilt a skirt

Notes: How did you feel today? (e.g. sleep, diet, etc.)

_____

_____

_____

_____

_____

Notes: How did the session go? (e.g. Improves/Goals for the next session)

_____

_____

_____

_____

_____

Notes:

_____

_____

_____

_____

_____

Week 10 - 2

Events	Distance/ Height	Best of 5	Worst of 5
Braemar			
Open			
LWFD			
HFWD			
L Hammer			
H Hammer			
WOB			
Shaef			
Caber (Turn)			

Drills ran today
(e.g. battle drill/pick and carry)

_____

_____

_____

_____

Grid Consistency/Volume Training

Events	Current PR	80%	# of Reps

Be happy while you're living, for you're a long time dead (*Scottish proverb*)

———◆◇◆———

Notes: How did you feel today? (e.g. sleep, diet, etc.)

_____

_____

_____

_____

_____

Notes: How did the session go? (e.g. Improves/Goals for the next session)

_____

_____

_____

_____

_____

Notes:

_____

_____

_____

_____

_____

Week 10 - 3

Events	Distance/ Height	Best of 5	Worst of 5
Braemar			
Open			
LWFD			
HFWD			
L Hammer			
H Hammer			
WOB			
Shaef			
Caber (Turn)			

Drills ran today
(e.g. battle drill/pick and carry)

Grid Consistency/Volume Training

Events	Current PR	80%	# of Reps

It's difficult to draw pure water
from a dirty well (*Scottish proverb*)

——————◆◇◆——————

Notes: How did you feel today? (e.g. sleep, diet, etc.)

_____

_____

_____

_____

_____

Notes: How did the session go? (e.g. Improves/Goals for the next session)

_____

_____

_____

_____

_____

Notes:

_____

_____

_____

_____

_____

Week 10 - 4

Events	Distance/ Height	Best of 5	Worst of 5
Braemar			
Open			
LWFD			
HFWD			
L Hammer			
H Hammer			
WOB			
Shaef			
Caber (Turn)			

Drills ran today
(e.g. battle drill/pick and carry)

_____

_____

_____

_____

Grid Consistency/Volume Training

Events	Current PR	80%	# of Reps

Today's rain is tomorrow's whiskey
(*Scottish proverb*)

Notes: How did you feel today? (e.g. sleep, diet, etc.)

_____

_____

_____

_____

_____

**Notes: How did the session go? (e.g. Improves/Goals
for the next session)**

_____

_____

_____

_____

_____

Notes:

_____

_____

_____

_____

Week 11 - 1

Events	Distance/ Height	Best of 5	Worst of 5
Braemar			
Open			
LWFD			
HFWD			
L Hammer			
H Hammer			
WOB			
Shaef			
Caber (Turn)			

Drills ran today
(e.g. battle drill/pick and carry)

_____

_____

_____

Grid Consistency/Volume Training

Events	Current PR	80%	# of Reps

Today's rain is tomorrow's whiskey
(*Scottish proverb*)

Notes: How did you feel today? (e.g. sleep, diet, etc.)

_____

_____

_____

_____

_____

Notes: How did the session go? (e.g. Improves/Goals for the next session)

_____

_____

_____

_____

_____

Notes:

_____

_____

_____

_____

_____

Week 11 - 1

Events	Distance/ Height	Best of 5	Worst of 5
Braemar			
Open			
LWFD			
HFWD			
L Hammer			
H Hammer			
WOB			
Shaef			
Caber (Turn)			

Drills ran today
(e.g. battle drill/pick and carry)

_____

_____

_____

Grid Consistency/Volume Training

Events	Current PR	80%	# of Reps

A willing mind makes a light foot
(*Scottish proverb*)

Notes: How did you feel today? (e.g. sleep, diet, etc.)

Notes: How did the session go? (e.g. Improves/Goals for the next session)

Notes:

Week 11 - 2

Events	Distance/Height	Best of 5	Worst of 5
Braemar			
Open			
LWFD			
HFWD			
L Hammer			
H Hammer			
WOB			
Shaef			
Caber (Turn)			

Drills ran today
(e.g. battle drill/pick and carry)

_____

_____

_____

_____

Grid Consistency/Volume Training

Events	Current PR	80%	# of Reps

Learn young, learn fair;
learn old, learn more (*Scottish proverb*)

Notes: How did you feel today? (e.g. sleep, diet, etc.)

_____

_____

_____

_____

_____

Notes: How did the session go? (e.g. Improves/Goals for the next session)

_____

_____

_____

_____

_____

Notes:

_____

_____

_____

_____

_____

Week 11 - 3

Events	Distance/ Height	Best of 5	Worst of 5
Braemar			
Open			
LWFD			
HFWD			
L Hammer			
H Hammer			
WOB			
Shaef			
Caber (Turn)			

Drills ran today
(e.g. battle drill/pick and carry)

_____

_____

_____

Grid Consistency/Volume Training

Events	Current PR	80%	# of Reps

When you fail at something, at least you're trying (*Scottish proverb*)

Notes: How did you feel today? (e.g. sleep, diet, etc.)

_____

_____

_____

_____

_____

Notes: How did the session go? (e.g. Improves/Goals for the next session)

_____

_____

_____

_____

_____

Notes:

_____

_____

_____

_____

_____

Week 11 - 4

Events	Distance/ Height	Best of 5	Worst of 5
Braemar			
Open			
LWFD			
HFWD			
L Hammer			
H Hammer			
WOB			
Shaef			
Caber (Turn)			

Drills ran today
(e.g. battle drill/pick and carry)

_____

_____

_____

_____

Grid Consistency/Volume Training

Events	Current PR	80%	# of Reps

Never let your feet run faster than your shoes
(*Scottish proverb*)

---◆◇◆---

Notes: How did you feel today? (e.g. sleep, diet, etc.)

_____

_____

_____

_____

_____

Notes: How did the session go? (e.g. Improves/Goals for the next session)

_____

_____

_____

_____

Notes:

_____

_____

_____

_____

Week 12 - 1

Events	Distance/ Height	Best of 5	Worst of 5
Braemar			
Open			
LWFD			
HFWD			
L Hammer			
H Hammer			
WOB			
Shaef			
Caber (Turn)			

Drills ran today
(e.g. battle drill/pick and carry)

_____

_____

_____

_____

Grid Consistency/Volume Training

Events	Current PR	80%	# of Reps

Where the stream is shallowest,
greatest is its noise (*Scottish proverb*).

———◆◇◆———

Notes: How did you feel today? (e.g. sleep, diet, etc.)

_____

_____

_____

_____

_____

**Notes: How did the session go? (e.g. Improves/Goals
for the next session)**

_____

_____

_____

_____

_____

Notes:

_____

_____

_____

_____

_____

Week 12 - 2

Events	Distance/ Height	Best of 5	Worst of 5
Braemar			
Open			
LWFD			
HFWD			
L Hammer			
H Hammer			
WOB			
Shaef			
Caber (Turn)			

Drills ran today
(e.g. battle drill/pick and carry)

_____

_____

_____

_____

Grid Consistency/Volume Training

Events	Current PR	80%	# of Reps

War makes thieves; Peace hangs them.
(*Scottish proverb*)

————◆◇◆————

Notes: How did you feel today? (e.g. sleep, diet, etc.)

_____

_____

_____

_____

_____

Notes: How did the session go? (e.g. Improves/Goals for the next session)

_____

_____

_____

_____

_____

Notes:

_____

_____

_____

_____

_____

Week 12 - 3

Events	Distance/ Height	Best of 5	Worst of 5
Braemar			
Open			
LWFD			
HFWD			
L Hammer			
H Hammer			
WOB			
Shaef			
Caber (Turn)			

Drills ran today
(e.g. battle drill/pick and carry)

_____

_____

_____

_____

Grid Consistency/Volume Training

Events	Current PR	80%	# of Reps

When everyone speaks, not everyone hears.
(*Scottish proverb*)

———————◆◇◆———————

Notes: How did you feel today? (e.g. sleep, diet, etc.)

_____

_____

_____

_____

_____

Notes: How did the session go? (e.g. Improves/Goals for the next session)

_____

_____

_____

_____

_____

Notes:

_____

_____

_____

_____

_____

Week 12 - 4

Events	Distance/Height	Best of 5	Worst of 5
Braemar			
Open			
LWFD			
HFWD			
L Hammer			
H Hammer			
WOB			
Shaef			
Caber (Turn)			

Drills ran today
(e.g. battle drill/pick and carry)

_____

_____

_____

_____

Grid Consistency/Volume Training

Events	Current PR	80%	# of Reps

Never complain, never explain

Notes: How did you feel today? (e.g. sleep, diet, etc.)

_____

_____

_____

_____

_____

Notes: How did the session go? (e.g. Improves/Goals for the next session)

_____

_____

_____

_____

_____

Notes:

_____

_____

_____

_____

_____

12-Month Highland Games Calendar

Use this calendar to keep track of the games you'd like to participate in and/or attend, as well as registration dates (registering for the event on registration day is encouraged as it can be competitive to get a spot).

You can also use the notes section to record PRs, goals, registration dates, etc.

JAN 01

S	M	T	W	T	F	S
					1	2
3	4	5	6	7	8	9
10	11	12	13	14	15	16
17	18	19	20	21	22	23
24	25	26	27	28	29	30
31						

FEB 02

S	M	T	W	T	F	S
	1	2	3	4	5	6
7	8	9	10	11	12	13
14	15	16	17	18	19	20
21	22	23	24	25	26	27
28						

JAN 01

_____

_____

_____

_____

FEB 02

_____

_____

_____

_____

MAR 03

S	M	T	W	T	F	S
	1	2	3	4	5	6
7	8	9	10	11	12	13
14	15	16	17	18	19	20
21	22	23	24	25	26	27
28	29	30	31			

APR 04

S	M	T	W	T	F	S
				1	2	3
4	5	6	7	8	9	10
11	12	13	14	15	16	17
18	19	20	21	22	23	24
25	26	27	28	29	30	

MAR 03

_____

_____

_____

_____

APR 04

_____

_____

_____

_____

MAY 05

S	M	T	W	T	F	S
						1
2	3	4	5	6	7	8
9	10	11	12	13	14	15
16	17	18	19	20	21	22
23	24	25	26	27	28	29
30	31					

JUN 06

S	M	T	W	T	F	S
		1	2	3	4	5
6	7	8	9	10	11	12
13	14	15	16	17	18	19
20	21	22	23	24	25	26
27	28	29	30			

MAY 05

_____

_____

_____

_____

JUN 06

_____

_____

_____

_____

JUL 07

S	M	T	W	T	F	S
				1	2	3
4	5	6	7	8	9	10
11	12	13	14	15	16	17
18	19	20	21	22	23	24
25	26	27	28	29	30	31

AUG 08

S	M	T	W	T	F	S
1	2	3	4	5	6	7
8	9	10	11	12	13	14
15	16	17	18	19	20	21
22	23	24	25	26	27	28
29	30	31				

JUL 07

_____

_____

_____

_____

AUG 08

_____

_____

_____

_____

SEP 09

S	M	T	W	T	F	S
			1	2	3	4
5	6	7	8	9	10	11
12	13	14	15	16	17	18
19	20	21	22	23	24	25
26	27	28	29	30		

OCT 10

S	M	T	W	T	F	S
					1	2
3	4	5	6	7	8	9
10	11	12	13	14	15	16
17	18	19	20	21	22	23
24	25	26	27	28	29	30
31						

SEP 09

_____

_____

_____

_____

OCT 10

_____

_____

_____

_____

NOV 11

S	M	T	W	T	F	S
	1	2	3	4	5	6
7	8	9	10	11	12	13
14	15	16	17	18	19	20
21	22	23	24	25	26	27
28	29	30				

DEC 12

S	M	T	W	T	F	S
			1	2	3	4
5	6	7	8	9	10	11
12	13	14	15	16	17	18
19	20	21	22	23	24	25
26	27	28	29	30	31	

NOV 11

_____

_____

_____

_____

DEC 12

_____

_____

_____

_____

It's a kilt and the answer is nothing.

Additional Resources

Official rules of the Highland Games:
http://www.shga.co.uk/cms/upload/file/SHGA%20
RULES%20OF%20COMPETITION_v19.10%282%29.pdf

Highland Games record holders:
http://www.highlandgames.net/records.html

ThrowBros
https://www.throwbros.com/

Governing Bodies

The Scottish Highland Games Association (SHGA):
http://www.shga.co.uk/

International Highland Games Federation (IHGF):
https://internationalhighlandgamesfederation.com/

Scottish Masters Athletics International (SMAI):
https://scottishmasters.org/

Southeastern Highland Athletics Group (SHAG):
http://www.throwshagshag.org/

MID-Atlantic Scottish Athletics (MASA):
http://www.heavyevents.com/

North American Scottish Games Athletics (NASGA):
http://www.nasgaweb.com/about.asp

Find Your Clan

You can use any of the following links to aid your journey
in finding your clan:
https://www.scotclans.com/scottish-clans/whats-my-clan/

https://clan.com/families

This one is especially helpful as it provides thousands of historical public records to help you discover your clan:

https://www.scotlandspeople.gov.uk/

Where to Buy a Kilt

Here are some links to places you can buy your kilt from.

USA Kilts:
https://www.usakilts.com/

SportKilt:
https://sportkilt.com/

UT Kilts:
https://www.utkilts.com/

Podcast

The Kilted Patriot:
https://anchor.fm/kiltedpatriot

Books

A Contrarian Approach to Highland Games by Mike and Mindy Pockoski

Throwing Lab by Matt Vincent

Heavy/Light: Periodized Throwing for the Highland Games by Mike Beech

ThrowHeavy: The Definitive Guide to the Scottish Highland Games by Daniel McKim

Kilted Patriot

Dedicated to living a virtuous and strenuous life, Gareth "The Kilted Patriot" Ainsworth, seeks to share what being an American means to him and to share his love of the Highland Games with the world. Follow him on social media:

https://www.instagram.com/kiltedpatriot/

And don't forget to tune in and subscribe to his podcast:

https://anchor.fm/kiltedpatriot

Author Bio

Gareth Ainsworth is a multi-faceted man — a husband, a father, a soldier, a friend, an athlete, a podcast host, a stoic, and a nature enthusiast. Gareth shares his experiences in what it means to be an American and strength sports, particularly the Highlan   d Games, on his podcast The Kilted Patriot, for those interested in the sport, the community, and the kilt.

Born in Wales and raised in the United Kingdom, Gareth later immigrated to the United States after meeting his wife. He has been serving in the US Army for ten years and has secured numerous qualifications under his belt, to include Advanced Mountain Warfare Training. Gareth became an American citizen on July 4, 2013, a milestone he celebrates with his family and friends every Independence Day.

He is incredibly passionate about the Highland Games and loves hiking, fishing, hunting, and exploring nature with his three children and wife. Gareth describes himself as a go-getter with a hunger for knowledge. He believes the only person stopping them from achieving something is themselves. Moreover, he loves motivating others to live a happier, healthier life.

Presently, Gareth is working as a recruiter in the US Army and acting as President of the 175th Infantry Regiment Association, a volunteer position. In the past, he has organized many fund-raising events to support military morale activities.

Gareth's passion and love for the Highland Games has encouraged him to write this book. He loves participating in the game, wearing a kilt, and being part of a community of like-minded individuals. In the future, he hopes to compete at The Arnold and in the A class of the Highland Games.

Made in the USA
Middletown, DE
15 July 2022

69439675R00099